362.883 Shuker-Haines,
SHU   Frances.   BRANCH

          Everything you
          need to know
          about date rape

$12.95

Everything You Need to Know About

DATE RAPE

Dating can be a good way to get to know people.

• THE NEED TO KNOW LIBRARY •

Everything You Need to Know About

DATE RAPE

Frances Shuker–Haines

Series Editor: Evan Stark, Ph.D.

THE ROSEN PUBLISHING GROUP, INC.
NEW YORK

Published in 1990 by The Rosen Publishing Group, Inc.
29 East 21st Street, New York City, New York 10010

First Edition
Copyright 1990 by The Rosen Publishing Group, Inc.

Manufactured in the United States of America.

Library of Congress Cataloging-in-Publication Data

Shuker-Haines, Frances.
      Everything you need to know about date rape.
      (The Need to know library)
      Includes bibliographical references.
      Includes index.
      Summary: Explains what date rape is, how to avoid it, and where to
find help if you're a victim.
      ISBN 0-8239-1075-X
      1. Acquaintance rape—United States—Juvenile
literature. [1. Acquaintance rape. 2. Rape.
3. Dating violence.] I. Title. II. Series.
HV6561.S56   1989
362.88'3—   89-10702
                                                                              CIP
                                                                              AC

Contents

Introduction

This book is about an important subject—date rape. Many people don't know very much about it. Some people have never heard of it. Date rape happens when two people go out together and the man forces the woman to have sex with him. Sometimes, a woman will force a man to have sex with her. This kind of date rape is rare. But it does happen. In the examples in this book a woman is the victim and a man is the rapist (except in Chapter 6: Guys Can Be Victims, Too). But if you're a guy, and you get raped, all the advice we give for girls who are raped will work for you.

Because the subject isn't talked about much, some girls don't even realize that they have been raped. They think that if a man forces them to have sex it must be their fault. Perhaps the man didn't understand their feelings, they think. Perhaps they should have behaved differently.

You will learn from this book that rape is never the victim's fault. If a man forces a woman to have sex with him, that's rape. This can be hard for a young girl to face. The date who raped her may be someone she has admired, or had a "crush" on. He may be someone she has never dated before, or he may be someone she knows very well.

In this book you will read a few stories about date rape. They will help you understand what date rape is. We will show you what kinds of thinking are behind a date rape. You will learn what goes on in the victim's mind. You will see how mixed messages lead to the tragedy of date rape.

Some things are easy to understand. If a girl is forced to have sex on a first date, that is rape. But a girl can be raped by a steady boyfriend, too. *Any* time a girl is forced to have sex, that is rape. Even if two people have had sex with each other before, if the man forces the woman to have sex, that's rape.

Remember that just because a girl has had sex with someone before, that doesn't mean she will want to have sex with every man she dates. And it doesn't mean she will want to have sex every time she goes out with someone. No one has a right to assume that sex will be part of a date, no matter who they go out with.

If two people go out together, they may decide they want to have sex. If they do not both want to have sex, and the man forces the woman, that is date rape.

If people respect each other's wishes and each other's feelings, date rape will not happen. This book will explain how misunderstandings about sex can happen, and how to avoid them.

When you know what can cause date rape, you will be able to protect yourself. You will learn what to do if you are raped. You will learn how to help rape victims. If you are a young man, you will learn how to avoid making the mistakes that lead to rape. Hopefully, we can all learn lessons that will make date rape a thing of the past.

If people respect each other's wishes and each other's feelings, date rape will not happen.

Chapter 1

What Is Date Rape, Anyway?

Rape. It's not a very pleasant subject. Most of us don't like to think about it. And when we do, we usually think of a stranger with a knife hiding in the bushes. He waits for a woman to walk by and then attacks. That's why a lot of us know not to walk alone after dark. But that's not the only kind of rape. Some rapes are "acquaintance rapes." That means the rapist and victim know each other. Eighty percent of all rapes are, in fact, acquaintance rapes!

One kind of acquaintance rape is called "date rape." This kind of rape happens when a man and a woman (or a teenage boy and girl) go out on a date together. The man forces the woman to have

sex with him when she doesn't want to. That sure
sounds like rape, doesn't it? *Any* kind of forced sex
is rape. But a lot of people don't see it that clearly.
They think rape only happens between strangers.
Or that if a woman was on a date, she must have
wanted sex. Or that the woman was "leading the
guy on." But any time a person has sex when he or
she doesn't want to, that's rape. A lot of people are
confused about date rape. They don't believe a
woman when she says she has been raped on a
date. They don't understand date rape. Why are
people so confused?

For teenagers, a lot of things about dating and
sex are hard to figure out. Boys aren't sure what
girls want. Girls don't know what boys want. Most
confusing of all, a lot of us don't know what *we*
want. This kind of confusion makes it hard to
understand date rape. But the definition is pretty
simple: If a girl doesn't want to have sex and a guy
makes her have sex with him anyway, it's rape.

A lot of people don't understand dating very
well. They have ideas about dating that aren't true.
These ideas make it hard to understand date rape.
See how many of these FALSE statements *you*
believe:

**When a woman says "no," she really means
"yes."** A lot of guys think a girl says no just
because she's supposed to. They think every girl
really wants sex and it's a guy's job to help her get

The victim needs support from friends who will believe her and listen to her problems.

it. But a guy doesn't have the right to make up a girl's mind for her. And he doesn't have the right to have sex with her against her will.

If a woman is flirting with a man, that means she wants to "go all the way." Everybody likes to flirt. Half the fun of a date is flirting. And the reason you date is to see if you two like each other. If you do, you might decide to have sex sometime in the future. But a guy can't make that decision by himself. Both people have to agree to have sex. Otherwise, it's rape.

If a woman goes somewhere alone with a man, that means she wants to have sex with him. Sometimes it's nice for a girl to be alone with her date. It's easier to talk and to find out what the guy's really like. They might want to see how they get along together without their friends around. But that doesn't mean the girl wants to have sex with her date. It only means that she wants to be alone with him.

If a man spends a lot of money on a date, the woman "owes" him something in return. People date because they like each other. They want to spend some time together. Dating *isn't* like a business deal. And sex is *not* something you pay for. A man and a woman may have sex after a date. But it should be something they both want to enjoy with each other.

You've probably heard some of these WRONG ideas. Now you can begin to understand how date rape happens. Date rape happens when one person decides what's best for both people.

Date rape causes many serious problems. One of these problems is how the victim of date rape feels about what has happened to her. Often, girls aren't even sure they have been raped. They think maybe they "asked" for it, even though they said "no." They think only strangers can rape them. They know they didn't have a choice about having sex. They feel that they were treated like a thing instead of a human being. And they can't believe someone they liked and trusted could do this to them. They start to feel that they can't trust *anyone*. What's worse, when they finally *do* tell someone what happened, that person may not believe them.

Victims of date rape are hurt
- By the rape
- By their own doubts about what happened
- By doubts of others about what happened

Why we need to know about date rape
- Girls must learn *not* to be victims
- Boys need to learn respect for girls
- Boys need to learn "no" means "no"
- We need to learn to help rape victims

Sometimes boys feel pressure to trade stories about girls.

Chapter 2

It Happened One Night . . .

Sandy liked Jeff a lot. He was very popular. He'd gone out with a lot of girls, and they were all pretty. The guys liked to swap stories about Jeff's success with girls. He was a real "ladies' man," all right.

Sandy often hung around after school with a group of her friends. They waited for Jeff and his friends to walk by. Then they would all talk and kid around and have fun. Sandy didn't know if Jeff noticed her or not. Sandy thought she was pretty. But she didn't know if she was pretty enough for Jeff. Sandy was really excited when Jeff sat next to her one afternoon and whispered, "Hey, want to go to the dance with me Friday night?" She'd been

hoping he would ask. Maybe this would be the
beginning of something. Maybe she would be Jeff's
new girlfriend! Sandy couldn't wait until Friday.

All that week, Sandy flirted with Jeff after
school. As far as Sandy could tell, they both
seemed pretty excited about their date. She just
hoped she wouldn't blow it somehow. Oh well,
nothing to do now but wait and see, she thought.

When Friday night rolled around, Sandy and her
friends headed out for the school. They were
meeting the guys there. Sandy had spent hours
trying on outfits. She finally felt pretty good about
how she looked. She just hoped Jeff would like
her too.

When they got to school, Jeff took one look at
her and let out a slow whistle. Sandy was
embarrassed. After all, their friends were there.
But she figured it was a compliment and she
should be flattered. She just smiled and blushed.
Jeff took her hand and led her inside.

The school gym was packed. The band was
playing full blast. Jeff was a great dancer. Sandy
was really enjoying dancing with him. A slow song
came on and Jeff pulled her close. She could smell
beer on his breath. The guys must have gone to
the lake before the dance and had a few. Sandy
didn't like beer much. But she figured, "boys will
be boys," as her mother used to say. She felt Jeff's
hands on her back, and then even lower. He was

pulling her toward him and pushing himself into her. It was kind of exciting. But it was kind of scary and embarrassing, too. Jeff was really pressuring her. Sandy started to feel more and more uncomfortable. After all, they were in the middle of the school! Her English teacher was right across the room!

Sandy started to pull away. Jeff looked in her eyes. "Relax," he said. "Don't be so uptight. Just enjoy yourself." But it wasn't that easy for Sandy. She wanted him to stop. But she couldn't bring herself to tell him. Then he might not want to date her again. Then she definitely *wouldn't* be his next girlfriend. At last, the song was over. Sandy rushed to the girls' room to find her best friend, Sarah. But she wasn't there. Oh well, at least Jeff really liked her, she thought. It was probably just the beer that made him act so bold in front of everybody.

Jeff was waiting for her outside the girls' room. "Let's get out of here. It's too crowded," he said. "But I'm supposed to go home with my friends," said Sandy. "I promised my parents." "Don't worry," said Jeff. "I'll get you home." "Well," said Sandy, "I really think I'd better find my friends. I should go home with them like I promised." "Hey don't you trust me?" asked Jeff. "I said I'd get you home, didn't I?" "Okay," said Sandy finally. She was a little worried about going

off alone with Jeff. But she didn't want their date
to end so soon.

So she took his hand, and they walked outside.
"Where are we going?" asked Sandy. "How about
the lake?" said Jeff. Sandy knew a lot of kids went
to the lake to make out. And it sure would be fun
to make out with Jeff. Wow, was he cute! "Okay,"
said Sandy. "Great," said Jeff. "I know a special
spot where no one will bother us."

When they got to the lake, Jeff led Sandy to a
patch of woods nearby. He sat down by a big
mossy tree trunk and pulled on Sandy's hand. She
lost her balance and landed smack in his lap. She
giggled a little at that. Jeff reached around the tree
and pulled out a six-pack of beer. "I hid these here
before the dance," he said proudly. So, Sandy
thought, he just assumed I'd come here with him!
She felt a little funny about that. Then she thought
maybe it was supposed to be a compliment. It
proved he really liked her.

Jeff opened two beers and handed her one. "Uh,
I don't really like beer," said Sandy. "You're
kidding!" said Jeff. "I don't believe you. Come on,
try it. Give it another chance." "Okay," said
Sandy. "But I don't think I'm going to like it."
Jeff started chugging his beer. Then he crushed the
can in his bare hand. He was definitely showing off
for her. He leaned over to kiss her. It was great.
Except for the beer on his breath, he was a really
good kisser. "Hey," he said between kisses.

Dancing close does not mean a girl wants sex.

"Where'd you learn to kiss like that?" Sandy couldn't believe it—he actually thought *she* was a good kisser. Amazing.

Pretty soon, Jeff started to put his hand under her sweater. Sandy wasn't sure she wanted him to do that, but she was afraid to say "no"and spoil the evening. So she let him. But then he started to get carried away. His hands were all over her. "Hey!" she said. "What do you think you're doing?" But he wouldn't stop.

Before she knew it, he was taking down her underpants. "Jeff, wait!" she said. "Come on, let's slow down." But he didn't seem to be listening. He got on top of her. "Jeff, stop!" cried Sandy. "Relax," he said. "You'll enjoy it."

"No, Jeff! Don't!" Sandy had never dreamed she would be having sex with Jeff. She barely knew him. She wasn't ready yet. She didn't have birth control. She just didn't *want* to.

"Jeff, please don't. Stop. Jeff? Please?" But all his weight was on her. He was inside her. It was over in a few seconds.

Sandy started to cry. "Hey, what's wrong?" said Jeff. "I thought we were having fun." Sandy was too stunned to say anything. She pulled her underpants up. Finally she managed to blurt out, "I want to go home now." "No problem," said Jeff. They walked home in silence. When they got to her front door, Jeff tried to kiss her. "You better not," said Sandy. "My dad's watching." "I'll call you," said Jeff. Sandy ran inside her house.

Sandy didn't tell anyone what had happened to her. She wasn't *sure* what had happened to her.

Why had Jeff gone ahead when she hadn't wanted him to? What had she done? Maybe she shouldn't have gone to the lake. But she'd wanted to kiss Jeff. Wasn't that all right? Maybe she shouldn't have kissed him so passionately. After all, maybe he just couldn't help himself. Maybe she shouldn't have let him put his hands under her sweater. But she knew that what he'd done after that had been wrong.

In her mind, she kept seeing Jeff on top of her. He barely knew she was there. She was just some *thing* to him. He didn't care about her. How could she have been so wrong about him? And how could she ever face him now? He'd acted like there was nothing wrong. *Was* she making something out of nothing? She was confused, unsure. Well, one thing was certain. She wasn't going to school on Monday. She just needed to be alone for a while to figure everything out.

When Sandy's friends called to ask her about her date, she lied. "Oh, it was fun," she said. She just couldn't bring herself to tell them what Jeff had done. Besides, she thought it might be her fault. She didn't want her friends to give her a hard time about being a "slut." But Sandy's best friend, Sarah, could tell that something was wrong. When Sandy didn't show up for school on Monday, Sarah got worried. She went to Sandy's house after school.

Sarah could tell Sandy had been crying. "Sandy, what happened? What's wrong?" asked Sarah.

"Nothing. I'm just not feeling well."

"What happened on Friday night? I expected you to call Saturday morning. Didn't it work out with Jeff?"At that, Sandy burst into tears, and told Sarah everything."What did I do wrong?"she asked.

"Nothing! Jeff is a jerk!" said Sarah.

"Why do I feel so terrible?" cried Sandy.

"I don't mean to shock you," said Sarah. "But it sounds to me like you've been raped."

And that is, in fact, what had happened to Sandy. She had been raped. But she had some trouble seeing it that way. She couldn't believe that someone she knew and trusted could rape her. She assumed that bad things don't happen to "nice" girls. So she blamed herself. But she was wrong. No one deserves to be raped. Victims should not be blamed for the crime that was committed against them.

Jeff assumed that Sandy wanted sex because she had been flirting with him. He also assumed she wanted sex because *he* wanted it. He assumed she wanted sex because she came to the lake with him.

But Jeff was wrong. If a woman says "no," she means "no." No one should ever force someone else to have sex against their will. That's rape. And rape is the fault of the rapist, not the victim.

Chapter 3

What Causes Date Rape?

Date rape happens when a man forces a woman to have sex when she doesn't want to. Why would a man do that? And why would a woman doubt that she was raped? Well, there are many reasons. Some of them have to do with the ways boys and girls are raised in this country.

In general, boys are taught to be more aggressive than girls. They are expected to enjoy playing sports. The rougher the sport being played, the more "macho," or "manly" they seem to others. Girls are expected to play less aggressive sports. Think about it: How many schools have girls' football teams?

Boys are sometimes taught that they should get their way, even if it means using violence. Girls are taught to stay away from conflict.

How many of you boys have been congratulated for winning a schoolyard fight? Now try to imagine a girl coming home with a bloody nose from a fight. Do you think her parents would say, "That's my girl!" and pat her on the back? It's not very likely. Chances are, her parents would be very concerned or very angry. Either way, they wouldn't approve of their little girl getting into a big fight.

Boys are sometimes taught to have a lot of girlfriends. They are taught not to get "tied down" by one girl when they're young. They are supposed to "play the field." Some boys think it is important to date pretty girls. If they date pretty girls, they'll look good to their friends. They'll seem a lot more "macho." Boys also think they are supposed to get a lot of sexual experience when they are in their teens and early twenties. They think this will also make them seem very manly.

Girls are often taught that they should have a steady boyfriend. They are taught to make themselves as pretty as they can. Then they can get a steady boyfriend more easily. They think that having a steady boyfriend will prove that they are "feminine."

Girls are sometimes taught to guard their "reputations." They are told that they should not be sexually active. They are taught that they will be seen as "easy" if others know they have had sex. Then no one will respect them, they are told.

Some boys think it is "macho" to date lots of girls.

All of these childhood "lessons" come into play in date rape. Date rape usually happens because the guy *expects* to have sex on the date. And he expects it because he thinks that "real men" have a lot of sex when they're young. Girls often resist having sex on a date. They have been taught that they shouldn't.

All through a date, the boy may ignore a girl's hints that she doesn't want sex. That way, he can keep assuming that the date will end in sex. Then, when it's clear that his date doesn't want to have sex, a guy might remember another "lesson" he has learned. He will use force to get his way.

Girls are often taught that they must be pretty and obedient to attract boys.

Otherwise, he tells himself, his friends will think he's a wimp.

Think about Jeff. All his friends admired him. They knew he had sex with lots of girls. It was important to Jeff to be a big shot to his friends. So, he clearly expected to have sex with Sandy. He planted the beer at the tree. He made sexual advances all night. He ignored her hints that she might be uncomfortable. He made sure the date ended in sex, even though Sandy said no. He assumed she didn't mean it. He assumed she didn't mean it because she had come to the lake with him. Jeff raped Sandy because of the "lessons" he'd learned about girls and boys and sex.

Many girls have learned things, too, that can lead to trouble. Girls want to please their dates. So they sometimes ignore their own wishes. Sometimes they have been taught to avoid "conflict." Sometimes they have been taught that they should not oppose a male's wishes. They may also have been taught to try to get men to like them. When a man goes too far, a girl might have a hard time saying no for these reasons. And when a man rapes her, she may assume it's her fault. Maybe she can't believe a nice guy would do this to her. She may also feel bad about herself. Maybe she was taught that only "easy" girls have sex.

Think about Sandy. She didn't want to dance so close to Jeff, but she was afraid to say no. She

thought if she said no, Jeff wouldn't like her. She
thought that it was her job to please Jeff. She
wanted to avoid conflict.

Sandy was surprised when Jeff pulled out the
beers. That meant that he just assumed she would
come to the lake with him. It meant that he
thought she didn't have a mind of her own. She
didn't like having no choice.

She also didn't like it when he put his hand
under her sweater. But instead of telling him, she
decided to pretend all these things were
compliments. She wanted Jeff to like her. When
Jeff raped her, she knew something bad had
happened. But she didn't blame Jeff at first. She
thought it must have been her fault. She thought
she must have "asked" for it. She couldn't believe
someone she liked and trusted could do this to her.

Movies, television, magazines and advertising
(known as the "media") also teach us "lessons"
about men and women that make date rape
possible. Many of these "lessons" are lies. Here are
some of the "lessons" or LIES we learn from the
media:

Women don't have minds of their own. Women
in movies and TV shows are often just something
nice to look at. The men are the ones fighting
crime or getting the bad guys. These men are often
surrounded by beautiful women. The women are

If a girl feels uncomfortable, she should speak up for herself.

something the men *have*—like a sports car or
expensive clothes—that shows everyone else how
great they are. These women are treated like
objects, not people. They are important because of
their looks, not because of their minds and
personalities. But women are not things. They are
human beings. They are important because of who
they are, not what they look like.

Women are sexual objects. Pornographic
magazines ("dirty" picture books) have nothing in
them but pictures of naked or nearly naked
women. In these magazines women are just things
to be looked at by men. The women in these
magazines are things that men look at for sexual
pleasure. They *can't* have minds and personalities.
They are just photographs. But they are considered
by many men to be "ideal" women. Pornographic
magazines teach men to think of women as their
sexual objects. But women are not sexual objects.
Women are people. Men cannot "use" them any
way they want to.

Women's bodies are products. Advertising also
treats women like objects. Pictures of beautiful
women are used to sell things. But the things have
nothing to do with the women in the ads. What do
cigarettes have to do with a woman's legs?
Nothing! The ads make you think you can "get"
this woman as easily as you get cigarettes. But

women's bodies are not things. You cannot buy a woman's body with an expensive dinner. Her body belongs to her. And a woman has the right to decide what she does with her body.

Movies, television, magazines and advertising are all around us. It's hard to remember that what they say about women isn't true. Men start to believe that women are supposed to be only pretty objects. They think that it is good to "have" women. They believe that having these pretty objects will make them more important. So, on a date, a guy might think of a girl as a thing instead of a person. He might think that he must "have" that thing to prove he's important. And since *things* can't say "no," a guy might ignore a girl when she does tell him to stop what he is doing.

Girls also believe some of the things the media say about them. They start to think it *is* more important to be pretty than to be smart. They think that will make them more worthwhile. So, on a date, a girl might have a hard time speaking up for herself. She may think that it's wrong to have opinions. She may think she's supposed to be an object of desire. When she's treated like an object, a woman finds out why that kind of thinking is wrong. Date rape happens because men treat women like objects.

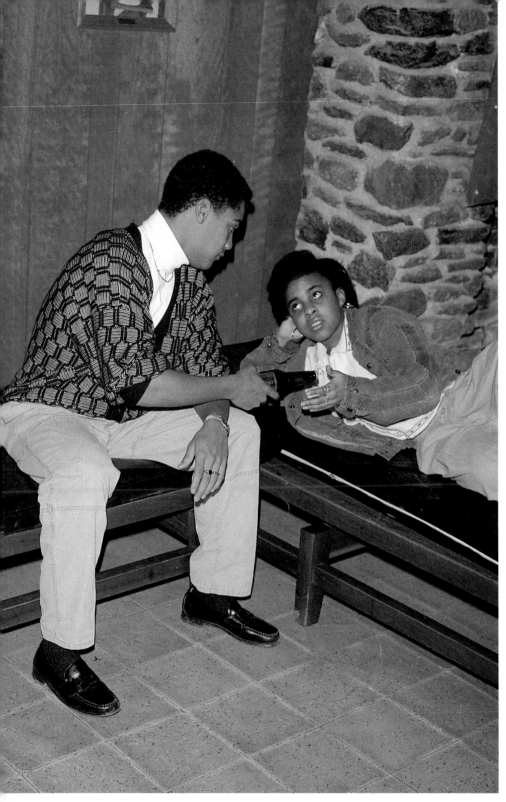

Just because a girl goes somewhere alone with a boy, it does not mean she wants to have sex with him.

Chapter 4

Girl Talk: How To Protect Yourself

The first thing to remember about date rape is this: It is never the victim's fault. We'll be talking about ways to protect yourself from date rape. But if it happens to you anyway (and it can), it is still *not your fault!*

You *can* reduce your chances of being a victim. That's what this chapter is about.

Let's think about Sandy's story first. Sandy is *not* responsible for the rape. But are there some things she could have done differently? Things that might have prevented the rape?

One thing Sandy could have done was *speak up for herself.* She didn't like what Jeff was doing during the slow dance. She pulled away from him, but then gave in. She also didn't feel very good about not going home with her friends. But she was afraid Jeff wouldn't like her. So she went along with him, even though it made her uncomfortable. She didn't like beer, but she let Jeff talk her into drinking some. She didn't want Jeff to put his hands under her sweater, but she let him anyway.

All night, Sandy did things she didn't really want to do. She did them to please Jeff. So when Jeff started to get on top of her and she said "no," it was the first time she acted like she really meant "no." The other times that night she said no at first, she gave in to Jeff. By the time Sandy tried to push him away, it was too late. Jeff assumed she'd go along with anything he wanted to do. After all, that's what had been happening all night. That doesn't mean Jeff was right. Jeff definitely raped Sandy. But if Sandy had *spoken up for herself* all night, her "no" might have been harder to ignore.

Sandy also could have *insisted they not go alone* to the lake. With other people around, Jeff might not have raped her. And she could have cried for help if he had tried. Going to the lake alone with Jeff might have given him the wrong idea. He might have thought she wanted to be alone so they could have sex. After all, that's why *he* wanted to go to the lake. Jeff was wrong to assume that Sandy wanted sex. But Sandy could have avoided the situation altogether if she'd *stayed with her friends*.

Date rape is much more likely to happen when people have been drinking. It makes the rapist less sensitive.

Sandy should have *made sure she had another way of getting home*. She was stuck with Jeff at the lake. He was the only one there who could take her home. Maybe if she'd had another way of getting home, she could have left when things got uncomfortable.

Another thing Sandy could have done is asked Jeff *not to drink alcohol.* Date rape is much more likely to happen when people have been drinking. It makes the rapist less sensitive. It makes him less aware of any hints his date is trying to give him. It makes him more likely to want to get his way.

Of course, even if he was drunk, Jeff is still responsible for what happened. But if he *hadn't been drinking,* he might have listened to Sandy. Sandy wasn't really drinking. That's good. When a date rape victim gets drunk, it's harder for her to defend herself. It's harder for her to control what's going on. But even if the victim is drunk, the rape is not her fault.

DANGER SIGNALS Sandy should have noticed:

Jeff ignored it
○ when she pulled away at the dance
○ when she wanted to go home with friends
○ when she said she didn't want beer
○ when she said "no" to sex

A guy may be capable of date rape if he
○ doesn't listen to your likes and dislikes
○ makes you nervous for fun
○ gets mad if you disagree with him

All these are signs that the guy doesn't respect you. Date rape is the ultimate disrespect.

Put yourself in Sandy's shoes on a date. Do you
○ go along against your will because it is "easier?"
○ keep quiet when a guy makes you uncomfortable?
○ worry if you don't go along the guy won't like you?

It's normal to say yes to these questions. But you have to change if you want to fight date rape. If a guy breaks up with you for standing up for yourself then he isn't worth dating. Remember when it comes to sex no one has the right to force you to do anything.

Chapter 5

For Guys Only: How To Stop Yourself From Hurting Girls

J ohn had been thinking about asking Maria out for months. He'd heard a lot of stories about her from the guys. It sounded like she'd had a lot of sexual experience. So, when he asked her out and she accepted, he was sure that they would end up sleeping together at the end of the date.

On the big night, he picked her up at her apartment. She was wearing very tight pants and high-heeled boots. She looked incredible! "Hi, John," she smiled, and gave him a kiss right on the mouth. Wow, the guys weren't kidding, thought John. She *is* hot! They decided to take a walk and then head out for a jazz club. While they were walking, Maria kept stroking his palm with

her fingers. Occasionally they'd stop and kiss.
Maria had this unbelievable way of nibbling on his
ear. By the time they got to the club, John was
super excited. He ordered a large frozen margarita.
Maria, he noticed, was only having Coca-Cola. Oh,
well, maybe she didn't *need* to drink, he thought.
This dating/sex thing is probably routine for her.
But he felt that he might lose his cool if he didn't
have something to calm himself down. By the time
the music was over, John had downed three
margaritas. He felt much more confident. He was
ready for the real excitement to begin.

He took Maria to his friend Freddie's
apartment—Freddie's parents were away for the
weekend. The minute they closed the door, Maria
was all over him. She was an incredible kisser.
They ended up on the floor. Well, now's my
chance, thought John. He started to undress
Maria. When he started unzipping her pants, she
whispered, "No, John. Not now. Let's save that
for another time." "Oh, I see," said John. "You're
playing hard to get. Well, you don't have to
pretend with me, Maria." "No, I mean it. Don't.
Let's just have fun doing what we're doing." John
was sure he knew what *that* meant. So he pulled
off her pants. "John, I said no," Maria repeated.
"Let's just kiss or something." "Yeah," said John.
"Or *something*!" He got on top of her. He *knew* she
didn't mean it. All the guys said she was easy.

It is important to treat your date with respect.

There was no way that she meant what she was saying. It was obvious that she'd been thinking about sex all night.

It was strange. The whole time he was having sex with her, she kept saying she didn't want to. She stopped kissing him. She was being really cold. And when they were through, she said, "I think I'd better be going," and before he knew it, she was out the door. What had gone wrong? Why hadn't she enjoyed the sex? And why did she keep saying no when it was so *obvious* that she was hot for him?

The fact is, John raped Maria, and didn't even know it. His head was so full with what he *thought* would happen, that he couldn't see what was really happening.

One of the strangest things about date rape is that sometimes men commit date rape without knowing what they've done. A burglar knows that he or she has stolen something. A car thief knows that he or she is taking someone else's car. A rapist in the bushes knows that he intends to rape someone.

But when it comes to date rape, things aren't that clear-cut. A lot of guys honestly believe the media stories we talked about earlier. They think that women really do mean "yes" when they say "no." They think that a woman must want sex if she goes somewhere alone with a guy. They think that if a girl flirts with a guy, she must want sex. They think that a girl owes a guy sex if he's spent a lot of money on her. So, when a guy like this forces his date to have sex, he may not even know he's raping her! He thinks he's just doing what guys are supposed to do on dates.

Well, we know better now. But let's think about ways we can be sure we don't make this kind of mistake in the future. For example, what could John in the story have done differently?

First of all, John could have *listened to his date*. When Maria said "no," he should have believed her and stopped—no matter how excited he was. It doesn't matter how sexy she acted. Or think about the first story. Jeff could have "listened" to Sandy's signals all night. When Sandy pulled away from him at the dance, Jeff should have asked if she was uncomfortable. When Sandy said she wanted to go home with her friends, he shouldn't have talked her out of it. Both John and Jeff made all the decisions. Maria and Sandy couldn't make any. That's not fair.

Another thing both John and Jeff could have done was *not drink alcohol*. When you're drunk, you can't think very clearly. You might not notice the hints your date is sending you. You might let yourself "get carried away." If you *stay sober*, you can avoid tragic mistakes like date rape.

John shouldn't have expected to have sex on the date. Date rape often happens because the guy

Calling a rape crisis counselor can help you understand what has happened.

expects to have sex long before the date even happens. Maybe he's been thinking about it for days. Maybe he's planned the whole evening so it will end up with sex. John asked Maria out just so he could have sex with her. He clearly expected to have sex with her. He "knew" that she would want it, long before he even asked her. Well, you can't make plans for two people all by yourself. *Don't expect sex from your date.* Try to enjoy whatever happens. Remember, the point of dating is to have fun, and to find out if you and your date really like each other. The point of a date is not rape. Don't let yourself be a rapist.

Don't let yourself believe the lies you see in the media. Women are just as important as men. When guys forget that, it can lead to date rape. Remember, women are people. They aren't just something pretty to look at or have. And how they look doesn't mean they are ready for sex. Just because Maria had on tight pants doesn't mean she wanted sex. Sure, she wanted John to be attracted to her, but that doesn't mean she wanted him to force sex on her. When you see those lies about women in the media, make a point of noticing. Talk about it with your friends—male and female. Think about most of the women you know. They're not like the women in magazines or on TV, are they? They have minds of their own. They have personalities and opinions. They are people, not things. They deserve respect.

Guys can also be pressured into having sex against their will.

Chapter 6

Guys Can Be Victims, Too

Michael was a good-looking guy who was shy with girls. He had entered school in the middle of the year because his parents moved. He missed his old girlfriend from his old home town. They had agreed to break up when he moved. But he was still in love with her. He couldn't imagine being with anyone else.

That's why Michael was really surprised when Kathy asked him out. She was captain of the girls' basketball team—tall, athletic, and very outgoing. "We were talking about you at practice the other day," she said. "We decided you were very mysterious. So, I thought I'd better find out for myself what you were all about." Michael was

flattered, but also very nervous. She was so
popular and pretty! Why did she want to go out
with *him?*

On their date they went to the movies. Then
Kathy invited him to her apartment. No one else
was home. She started coming on very strong,
kissing him, stroking him. She was very hard to
resist. "Well, the girls were right," she said. "You
do have great lips!" She laughed.

Were they really talking about me this way,
thought Michael? Wow! Kathy guided his hand
under her shirt. Michael couldn't help himself—he
started thinking about his old girlfriend and how
much he missed her. Sure, it was nice being with
Kathy, but he barely knew her. Before he knew it,
Kathy was taking off his clothes and her clothes,
scattering them around the room. Michael was
suprised. Did this mean she wanted to have sex?
He wasn't ready for that. He was still in love with
his old girlfriend. *That's* who he wanted to be with,
not Kathy.

"Um, Kathy," he stammered. "Do you think
this is a good idea?" "Oh, give me a break,
Michael. I'm giving you a chance of a lifetime!
What's the problem?" She was laughing at him.
"Well, I don't want to do this," he said. "I'm just
not into it right now." "Oh, come *on*," she said.
"You've got to be kidding!" And before he knew
it, she was all over him. "What's the matter,

Michael? You gay or something?" She laughed again.

They had sex. And Michael felt terrible afterwards. He hadn't wanted to, and she had made him do it. He felt kind of hollow inside. This wasn't how he had always imagined it would be.

Believe it or not, Kathy raped Michael. Anyone—man or woman—who forces another person to have sex against his or her will has committed rape. But it's especially confusing for guys. They're supposed to want sex *all* the time. They're supposed to be the aggressive ones. So when they're forced to have sex, they have a hard time figuring out what happened. They think they *must* have wanted it. They think they must have been responsible in some way. But, as you can see from the story, that isn't always the case. Men can be raped, too. If this ever happens to you, the advice in this book can be used for guys, too. If you think you've been raped, chances are you aren't crazy, you're just a victim. And you need help. This book will tell you how to get the help you need.

Anyone—man or woman—who forces another person to have sex against his or her will has committed rape.

Rape victims often feel alone. They blame themselves.

Chapter 7

What If It Happens To You?

If you are a victim of date rape, you will probably feel very confused and upset. A lot of different thoughts will be running through your head. Here are some of the things you might find yourself wondering:

How could this happen to me?

Sometimes we don't want to believe that something so horrible could happen to us. We try to find a reason for it. Rape victims often blame themselves. They think they must have done something wrong. That isn't true. It's not your fault if you were raped. It is the rapist's fault. You can (and should) be angry with him. Don't be angry with yourself.

How could he have done this to me?

We date people we think we like. We date people we think are nice. That makes it hard to believe that something as horrible as rape really happened. But even guys you think are nice can rape. There was no way for you to know what was going to happen. It's not your fault that your date ignored your wishes. *He's* the one at fault.

How can I ever trust anyone else again?

You trusted your date. He raped you. It's hard to feel good about people after an experience like that. But just because one person is bad doesn't mean that *everyone* is bad. Maybe there were some danger signals you didn't pick up on. Now you'll know what to look for. Remember, most people are good. There are still a lot of people you can trust.

How can I ever trust myself again?

You might feel that you made a terrible mistake. You trusted someone you shouldn't have. You liked someone who was mean to you. This may make you feel that you can't do anything right. You might start to feel that any decision you make will be wrong. But it wasn't your fault that someone you liked did something bad. And it doesn't mean that you're stupid. You were a victim. A crime is never the victim's fault.

Don't be surprised if you feel upset for a long time. Rape is a terrible thing. It takes a long time to feel good about the world again. It takes a long time to feel good about yourself again.

Here are some things you can do to help yourself feel better:

One thing that will help is *talking to someone* right away. Even if you're not sure what's happened to you, you should get help. Sandy, for example, was very confused and upset. But she kept it to herself. That only made it worse.

The problem is, not everyone you talk to will be helpful or supportive. Sometimes parents or friends don't understand about date rape. They may think that it was your fault. Or that you "just got carried away." Or they may be upset at the idea of your having sex. So, try to talk to someone you're pretty sure will understand.

You can also *call a rape crisis center*. The person who answers the phone is an expert on rape. He or she will always believe you. Rape crisis counselors know all about date rape.

You can get the phone number of a rape crisis center by looking in the phone book under "Rape." Be sure to check both the white pages and the yellow pages. Or you can call the operator and ask to talk to a rape crisis center. When you call the rape crisis center, you can talk about anything you want. The counselor you talk to will never tell anyone what you said unless you want them to.

Rape is against the law. You may decide you want to report your rape to the police.

The counselor will stay on the phone with you as long as you want. The counselor will help you *figure out exactly what happened to you.* She or he can give you advice about finding other people to talk to—a therapist, a minister or rabbi, a sympathetic friend, a parent.

Your rape crisis counselor can also help you *decide about going to the police.* Rape is against the law. You may decide you want to report your rape to the police. You may decide you want to take your case to court. It's your decision. If you decide to go to the police, your rape crisis counselor will be able to tell you what to expect.

Don't be surprised if the police aren't as sensitive as the rape crisis counselor. The police don't know as much about date rape as the counselor does. If the police upset you, call the rape crisis center. They will help you cope.

Another way to get help is to *go to the hospital.* People in the emergency room can help gather evidence and treat any wounds. Often, there is a social worker or counselor you can talk to at the hospital. Sometimes a police officer will be there. If you're still upset after you leave, call the rape crisis center.

You might also talk to someone at the hospital or the rape crisis center about *medical tests*. You might have been given a sexually transmitted disease. You might be pregnant. You will need to get medication or counseling right away.

You may also want *legal help*. Again, your rape crisis counselor can tell you where to go. But don't be surprised if a lawyer tells you that it will be hard to win your case. Date rape is hard to prove in court. That's because a lot of people still don't understand date rape. But that's changing.

Recovering from date rape isn't easy. You will probably be upset for a long time. You will have a lot of decisions to make—who to tell, what to do. Do things that you know will make you feel better. Find people you feel safe talking to. If one person isn't being sympathetic, talk to someone else. If one person gives you advice that makes you uncomfortable, go to someone else. If someone tries to blame you for what happened, go to someone else. If someone tells you to just "forget it," go to someone else. Your recovery is more important than someone else's feelings. Don't worry. If they really care about you, they'll get over it.

If date rape happens to you, you'll need help. Make sure you get it.

If a friend has been raped, she may need you to listen.

Chapter 8

How To Be A Friend In Need

If someone you know is raped, they will need lots of help. As a friend, you can make a victim's recovery a lot easier. Here are some ways to do that.

First of all, believe her.

People sometimes don't believe that date rape is really rape. They think only strangers can rape you. They think the victim must have "asked" for it. They think the victim must have done something wrong or the guy wouldn't have "taken advantage" of her. Well, none of these things are true. And it hurts when no one believes you. Your job is to believe your friend. If she feels she was raped, she was raped. Don't question it. Just be supportive.

Listen—a lot!

Date rape victims have a lot of confusing feelings. Talking about those feelings will help a victim to cope with them. She may need to talk about it for a long time. She may need to talk about it more as time goes by. You don't need to say much. She just needs to know you're there.

Know how to get help.

If your friend tells you she's been raped, find out what she's done about it. If she hasn't called a rape crisis center, encourage her to. If she's been injured, suggest she go to the hospital. If she wants to go to the police, help her get advice at a rape crisis center first. Date rape is very upsetting. Your friend will probably need some help getting help. You can help her do that.

Support her decisions.

If your friend doesn't want to go to the police, don't make her. If she does want to go to the police, help her do that. Date rape makes you doubt your judgment. Friends should support a victim's decisions. This will make the victim feel more in control. It will make her feel more

The rape may even have happened years ago. But when the victim realizes what happened to her, she will need help.

confident. Don't try to force your friend to do anything. That will only make her think she *really* can't make decisions for herself.

It takes some date rape victims a long time to realize that they were raped. The rape may even have happened years ago. But when the victim realizes what happened to her, she will need help. She will need just as much support as someone who was raped more recently. Be the same kind of good friend to this kind of victim, too.

It's not easy to help a friend through a crisis. Especially when the crisis is something as awful as date rape. So be sure that *you* have support, too. Let someone know what *you're* going through. Otherwise, you might get upset and overwhelmed. Then you can't be a good friend. And if you feel that you're in over your head, get some advice from a rape counselor. She or he will tell you what to do next. You don't have to do this alone. Take care of yourself so you can take care of your friend.

Chapter 9

What Have You Learned?

Date rape is pretty easy to define. When a guy forces his date to have sex with him, that's date rape.

A lot of people are confused about date rape. They believe a lot of myths (stories) about dating that just aren't true.

○ They believe that *only strangers can rape.*

○ They believe that *when a woman says "no," she really means "yes."*

○ They think that *if a woman flirts with a man, that means she wants to have sex with him.*

○ They believe that *if a woman goes somewhere alone with a man, that means she wants to have sex with him.*

○ They believe that *if a man spends a lot of money on a date, the woman owes him something.*

NONE OF THESE MYTHS ARE TRUE.
Believing them can lead to date rape.

A lot of people blame the victim of date rape. They think she must have done something wrong, or the guy wouldn't have raped her. This makes the victim feel even worse. First, she was raped. Then, no one believed her. This makes her pain twice as bad.

Date rape happens for a lot of reasons. Boys and girls are taught certain things as children. Boys are taught to be aggressive. Girls are taught to be passive. This combination can lead to the tragedy of date rape.

The media make us believe that women are objects. Date rape happens when a man treats a woman like a sexual object.

There are things we can do to prevent date rape. Girls can learn to speak up for themselves. They can learn the danger signals that say "stay away from *this* guy!" Guys can learn to be more sensitive to the signals their dates are sending them. They can learn that respecting their date is more important than having sex with her.

A girl who has been raped *can* do something about it. There are people she can talk to. There are legal steps she can take. She can learn more about date rape. She can learn that it wasn't her fault.

We can all learn to help friends who have been raped. We can believe them. We can listen to them. We can find professional help for them. Helping our friends heal will make us *all* better people.

Date rape is a tragedy. But it's a preventable tragedy. If you're a girl, take steps to protect yourself. If you're a guy, treat your dates with respect. Remember that "no" means "no." Now that you know how to prevent date rape, spread the word. Make sure that date rape doesn't happen to anyone you know.

Glossary—*Explaining New Words*

aggressive   Pushy; being forceful to get what you want.

date rape   Forcing someone who is not a stranger to have sex.

feminine   Like a woman, gentle.

macho   Like a "he-man"; tough.

media   Newspapers, magazines, television, movies, radio, etc.

passive   The opposite of aggressive; giving in to others.

rape   Sex against someone's will.

rape crisis center   A place where rape victims can get help.

rape crisis counselor   A person trained to help rape victims.

sexual object   Something that exists only for sexual pleasure.

victim   A person who has a crime committed against them.

Where To Get Help

Rape Crisis Centers
To find one, look in the phone book under Rape (check both white and yellow pages). Or call the operator or a suicide-prevention hotline. They will help you get in touch with a rape crisis center.

Hospital Emergency Room
Ask if they have a Rape Trauma Team. This is a team of people who have special training in coping with rape.

The Police
Dial 911 on any phone.

The YWCA
Look in the phone book or call information for the number. The YWCA can help you find a rape crisis center. Many also run self-defense programs.

For Further Reading

Bateman, Py. *Acquaintance Rape: Awareness and Prevention for Teenagers.* Seattle: Alternatives to Fear, 1982, 24 pages. This book emphasizes prevention of acquaintance rape: how to identify "red-flag" behavior, and what to do about it.

Bateman, Py. *Macho: Is That What You Really Want?* Seattle: Alternatives to Fear, 1986, 48 pages. This book is just for boys, to help them fight negative peer pressure and learn new ways to relate to girls.

Benedict, Helen. *Recovery: How to Survive Sexual Assault for Women, Men, Teenagers, and Their Friends and Families.* New York: Doubleday, 1988, 293 pages. This book takes the reader through every step of the recovery process for every kind of rape. Includes useful resources and lots of practical information for victims.

Benedict, Helen. *Safe, Strong and Streetwise: The Teenager's Guide to Sexual Assault.* Boston: Joy Street Books, 1986, 192 pages. This book tells how to practice "sexual safety" in a variety of situations that teens might find themselves in.

Parrot, Andrea. *Coping With Date Rape and Acquaintance Rape.* New York: The Rosen Publishing Group, 1988, 118 pages. This book examines every kind of date and acquaintance rape, explaining its causes and the devastating effects it can have on its victims.

Index

About the Author
Frannie Shuker-Haines is a free-lance writer currently living in Ann Arbor, Michigan. She specializes in writing about parenting and child rearing.

About the Editor
Evan Stark is a well-known sociologist, educator, and therapist as well as a popular lecturer on women's and children's health issues. Dr. Stark was the Henry Rutgers Fellow at Rutgers University, an associate at the Institution for Social and Policy Studies at Yale University, and a Fulbright Fellow at the University of Essex. He is the author of many publications in the field of family relations and is the father of four children.

Acknowledgments and Photo Credits

Photos by Stuart Rabinowitz

Design/Production; Blackbirch Graphics, Inc.
Cover Photo by Stuart Rabinowitz